I have
CYSTIC FIBROSIS

I have CYSTIC FIBROSIS

Brenda Pettenuzzo
meets
Victoria Haines

Photography: Chris Fairclough

Consultant:
The Cystic Fibrosis Research Trust

FRANKLIN WATTS
London/New York/Sydney/Toronto

Victoria Haines is twelve years old. She has Cystic Fibrosis. Her parents are both Chemistry lecturers at a London Polytechnic. Victoria is an only child, and she lives with her parents near the London/Essex borders. She is a pupil at Woodford County High School.

Contents

Early life	6
Daily routine	8
School	17
Raising money	21
Holidays	23
Facts about Cystic Fibrosis	27
The Cystic Fibrosis Research Trust	30
Glossary	31
Index	32

© 1988 Franklin Watts
12a Golden Square
LONDON W1

ISBN: 0 86313 746 6

Series Consultant: Beverley Mathias
Editor: Jenny Wood
Design: Edward Kinsey

Typesetting: Keyspools Ltd

Printed in Great Britain

The Publishers, Photographer and author would like to thank Victoria Haines and her family for their great help and co-operation in the preparation of this book.

Thanks are also due to Woodford County High School and to the Cystic Fibrosis Research Trust.

Brenda Pettenuzzo is a Science and Religious Education Teacher at St Angela's Ursuline Convent School, a Comprehensive School in the London Borough of Newham.

Early life

"I inherited Cystic Fibrosis from both my parents, just as I inherited the colour of my eyes, but they didn't know I had it at first."

Many people in Great Britain carry the Cystic Fibrosis gene. It has no effect on them at all. But if two people who both carry the CF gene have a child, then both genes might be passed on to that child and he or she will have CF. This is what happened to Victoria. Neither of her parents knew that they were carrying the gene until doctors told them Victoria had Cystic Fibrosis.

"My parents could tell that there was something wrong with me, but I was nearly two before they found out what it was."

Every person with Cystic Fibrosis is different. It isn't always easy to tell if a baby has it. Victoria's parents could tell that she wasn't digesting her food properly. They didn't know if anything else was wrong. The specialist doctor at their local hospital arranged for a special test to be done. This is called a "Sweat test". It proved that Victoria had Cystic Fibrosis. Since then she has been under the care of the local hospital, and goes for regular check-ups.

Daily routine

"Soon after I get up each morning I have to do my 'physio'. My mum usually helps me to get at the places I can't reach."

People who have Cystic Fibrosis produce a very thick type of mucus in their lungs. If they do not try to remove it, the mucus can make it hard for them to breathe. They can also get serious infections in their lungs. Physiotherapy, or "physio", can help to loosen the mucus. Victoria gets into various positions, and either she or her mum or dad has to "bang" her chest and back. The banging has to be done in a special way so that it doesn't hurt. The physiotherapist at the hospital showed Victoria's parents how to do it. She has "physio" each morning and evening, and more often if she catches a cold.

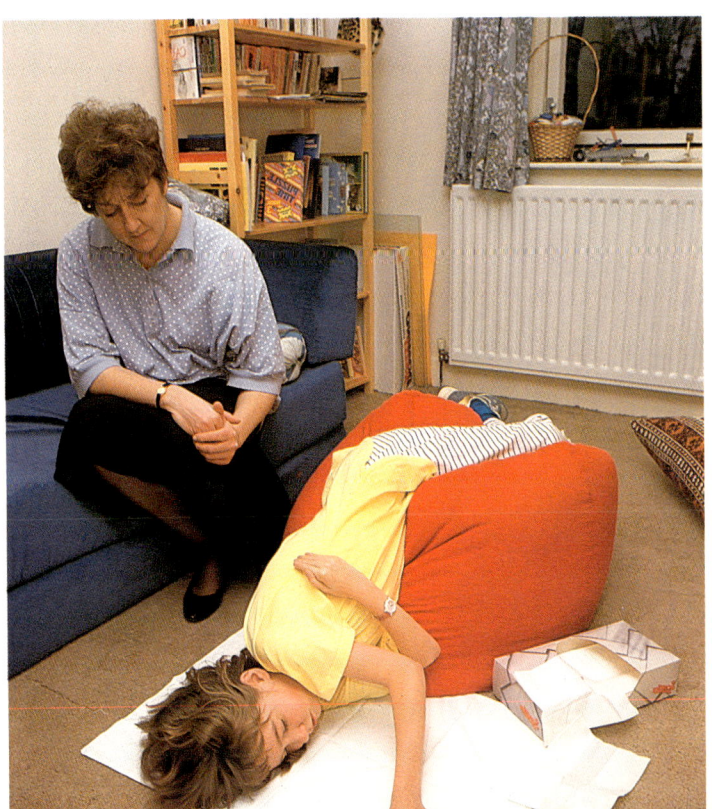

"After I have done my 'physio', I usually jump up and down on the trampoline for a while."

Exercise is very good for people with Cystic Fibrosis. It helps to keep their lungs clear. After a few jumps, Victoria always has to cough. This shows that she is loosening the mucus in her lungs. She uses the trampoline twice a day. Sometimes she uses the exercise bike as well, especially in bad weather when she hasn't been out of the house very much.

"A few years ago I learned how to do 'huffs'. They are another good way to help clear my chest."

"Huffing" is a method of forcing air out of the lungs. To do it, Victoria takes a normal breath then tries to force all the air out of her lungs, taking slightly longer than normal to do so. After a few "huffs", Victoria will need to cough hard to get the mucus out of her lungs. This is a more effective method of clearing the lungs than coughing alone.

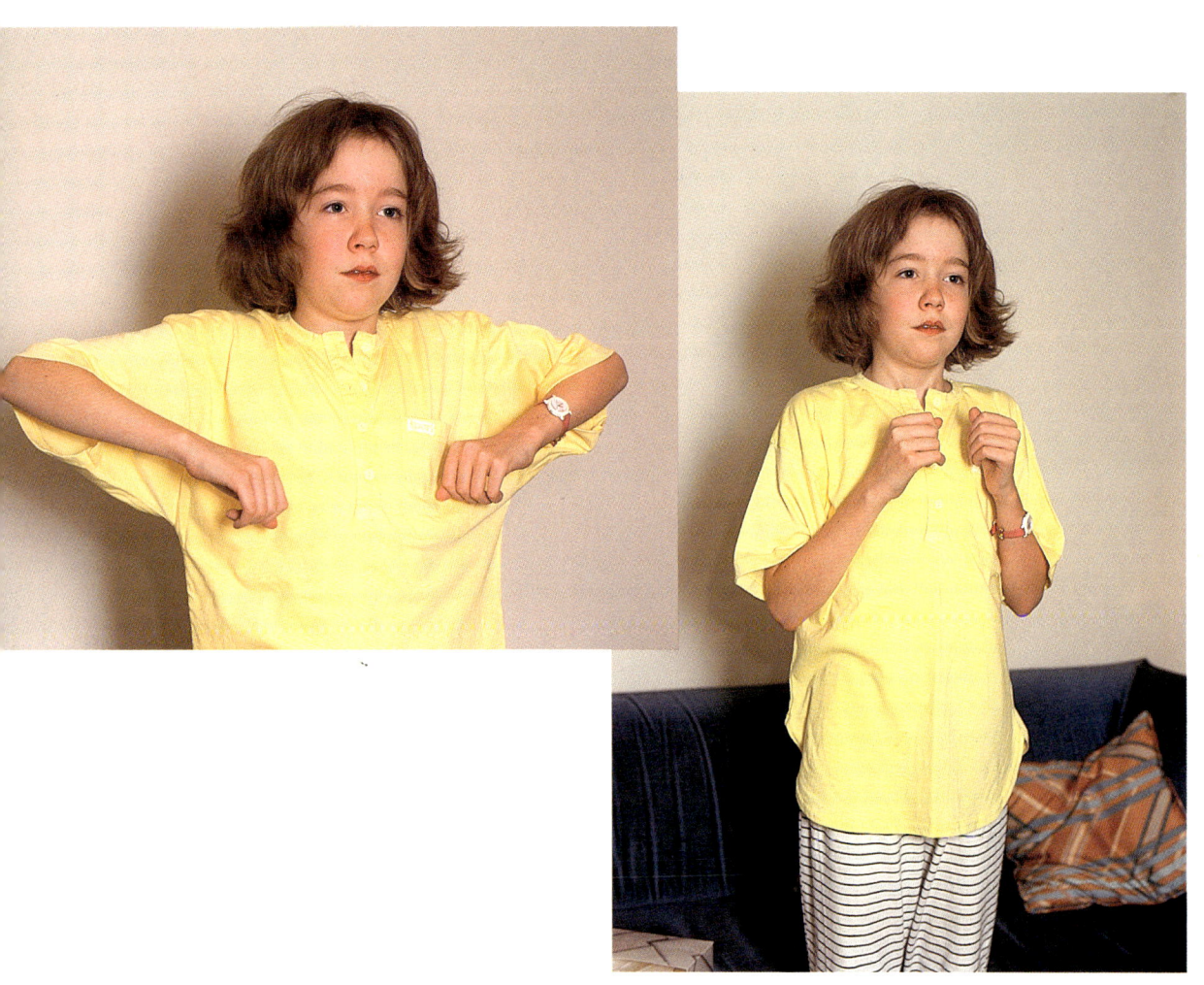

"I've always had to cough a lot. It's not infectious like an ordinary cough. It's the only way to clear my lungs."

Sometimes people think that boys and girls like Victoria need some treatment to stop their cough! Nothing could be further from the truth. Every time Victoria coughs, she is removing the thick mucus which her lungs produce. If it stayed there, it could cause serious damage to her lung tissue. The mucus which is coughed up is called "sputum". Changes in the appearance of the sputum are usually signs of chest infection.

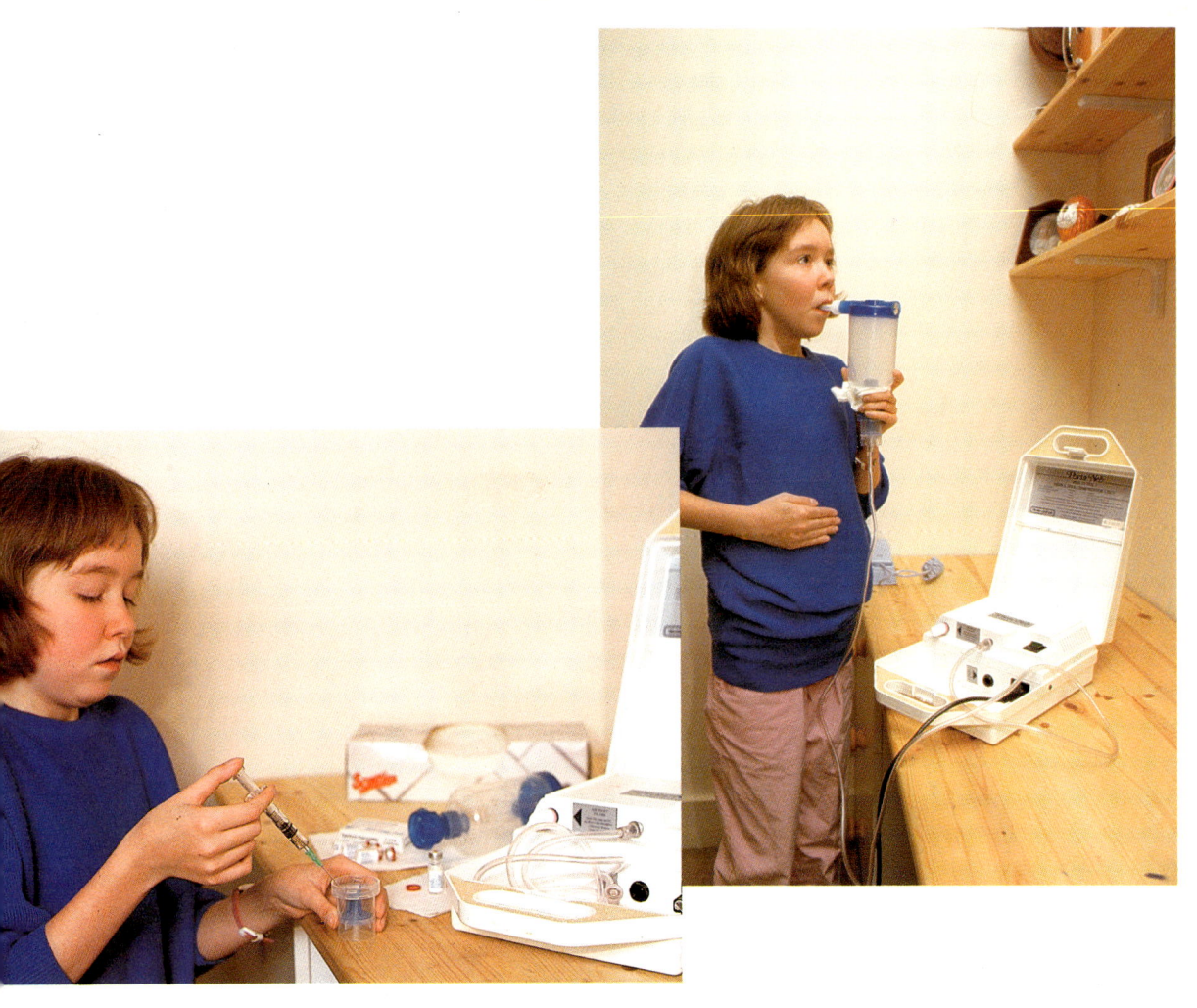

"Another thing which I have to do each day is to use my nebuliser."

Certain germs grow extra well in the lungs of people who have Cystic Fibrosis. Victoria has regular doses of antibiotics to prevent her from getting infected with these germs. Using a nebuliser is a very good method of getting the antibiotic into her lungs. It converts the antibiotic into a fine mist which can be inhaled through the face mask.

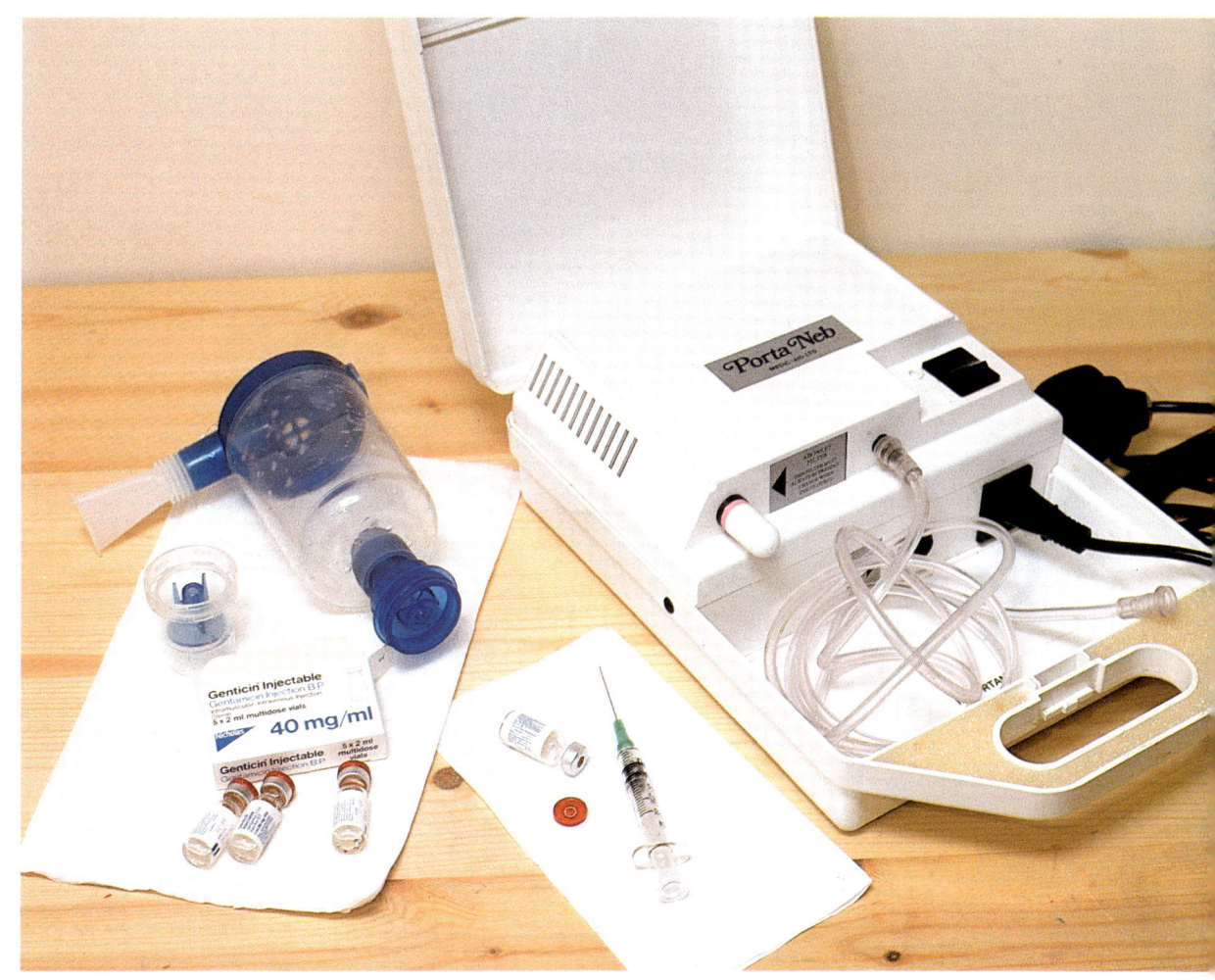

"I used to have a nebuliser which belonged to the hospital, but now I have my own portable one. It was very handy during the power cut!"

Setting up the nebuliser is quite complicated. Victoria can now do it for herself. This means that she can go anywhere and use it. If there is no electricity supply, she can use a car battery to make it work. She has several other medicines which she sometimes has to take, but she always uses the nebuliser twice a day.

"When I was younger there were lots of things I couldn't eat. I have a lot more fun now!"

People who have Cystic Fibrosis have problems with digestion. Extra-thick secretions in their digestive organs prevent them from digesting much of what they eat. Fats are especially difficult to digest. When Victoria was younger, she had to have a low-fat diet. This meant that she always had to take a packed lunch if she went out. She often took her own tea when she went to birthday parties! Another problem was giving her enough food to supply her with the energy she needed to stay healthy and grow properly.

"I can eat nearly everything now, as long as I take my capsules."

Victoria has capsules which contain digestive enzymes. These are the chemicals which help break down the food we eat so that it can be absorbed and used. She decides how many capsules she needs. If she is eating something which contains little fat, she might have only one capsule. If she is having something very fatty, she might need three or four or more of them.

"These capsules are very new, and they work in a very clever way."

The latest type of enzyme capsules contain three sorts of digestive enzymes. They are in the form of granules which have a special coating. This coating protects the enzymes from being destroyed in the stomach before they get to where they are needed. People who have Cystic Fibrosis who use these capsules are able to absorb much more of the fat and protein they eat than was previously possible.

School

"I am the only girl at my school who has Cystic Fibrosis."

When she was at primary school, and diet was more of a problem, Victoria used to take a packed lunch. This made her a little different from the other children. Now she has a school lunch, and there is very little about her to make her seem different from her fellow pupils. She does everything that the other girls do.

"I'm always hungry at break time. My friends and I always have a snack before we do anything else."

People who have Cystic Fibrosis always have absorption problems. However much they eat, they never absorb all of it through their digestive system. It is important for Victoria to eat as often as she can. She needs extra energy to keep her body well. This is even more important now, because she is at the age when most young people begin their teenage growth spurt.

"I enjoy lots of sports at school, both indoors and outside. I'm in the school table-tennis team."

Exercise is good for everyone who has Cystic Fibrosis. It is fortunate that Victoria enjoys so many sports, and that she gets the opportunity to take part in them. She gets so much practice in some games that it is difficult for her to find new partners. Her friends are afraid that she will become too hard to beat!

"A lot of people are surprised to learn that I can play the trumpet."

Although it is not surprising to hear that Victoria likes music, the trumpet is an unusual instrument for someone who has Cystic Fibrosis to play. It takes a great deal of effort to get a sound out of the instrument. But Victoria does everything she can to keep her lungs healthy. All the exercise she does has helped to make her chest muscles very fit. She has learned to play the trumpet in school, and she plays quite often at home.

Raising money

"I have managed to persuade my school to raise money for the Cystic Fibrosis Research Trust."

Each year, Victoria's school chooses which charities it will help by its fund-raising activities. Girls who have a special charity stand up in front of the whole school and talk about that charity. They have to persuade everyone else that their charity is worth supporting. Victoria has done this twice. Each time she has been successful. She has also raised money at home by holding a "garage sale" and has raised money for other charities at school by doing a sponsored swim.

"Each year when the Cystic Fibrosis Research Trust has a Flag Day, my parents and I help to collect money."

When her parents were told that she had Cystic Fibrosis, her father remembered that he had seen an advertisement on the London Underground for the Cystic Fibrosis Research Trust. He looked for the advert again and made a note of the phone number. Her parents phoned the Trust, and were put in touch with a local group. They have been involved with it ever since, and help out whenever possible, especially with fund-raising.

Holidays

"At weekends I usually make my dad play squash with me, or tennis in the summer."

Sometimes young people who have Cystic Fibrosis find it very difficult to keep up the daily routine of "physio", inhalations and diet. They know that they need to do these things to stay healthy, but they dislike *having* to do them. Victoria is lucky because she likes the exercise which she needs, and her parents are able to enjoy the sports with her.

"I used to be a Brownie, and now I belong to the local Guides."

The Guides meet every Friday, and Victoria rarely misses a meeting. As a Brownie she sometimes went on outings. Now that she is a Guide, she will be able to go away to camp. She will be able to follow her usual routine each morning and evening, using her portable nebuliser. She has already gained two badges, Hostess and Fitness, and hopes to work for more.

"Last year I was able to visit Canada with a group of young people who all have Cystic Fibrosis."

Victoria's holiday was arranged through a Cystic Fibrosis holiday charity. A group of thirty children and young people flew to a summer camp near Toronto. There were Camp Counsellors, doctors and nurses. All sorts of activities and trips were organised. Everyone had a great time, and Victoria was very sorry when the holiday came to an end. She was glad to see her mum and dad again, though, after four weeks away!

"I usually have my holiday a little closer to home. My parents and I often go away in our caravan."

Victoria and her parents are very close. Because she is an only child, they used to worry that she might be lonely when they went on holiday. When they take their caravan, Victoria quickly makes friends with other children at the same place. Even though she suffers from a serious disease, she manages to live a very active and fulfilled life.

Facts about Cystic Fibrosis

Cystic Fibrosis is an inherited disease. It is caused by the presence of a recessive gene. This means that the gene must have been passed on from both parents for a child to be affected. People who have only one affected gene are said to be "carriers" of CF and are generally unaware of its presence. Only when a carrier and his or her partner have a child is there a chance of that child having CF. Approximately 1 in 20 people in the UK are carriers of CF. When two carriers have a child there is a 1 in 4 chance of that child inheriting both genes and having CF. This chance operates for each pregnancy: some couples never have a CF child, and so are unaware that they are both carriers. In other families, all children may be affected.

It is thought that the CF gene only occurs in Caucasian (White Indo-European) people. On average, in most parts of the world, between 1 in 1500 and 1 in 2500 Caucasian children are born with CF. In the UK this means that an average of one child per day is born with CF, and four to five daily in the USA. Occasionally children of Pakistani or Arab descent are born with CF but it is virtually unheard of in children of Chinese or African Negro origins.

CF is not always evident at birth, and some children are not diagnosed for some time afterwards. When a baby is found to have CF, its older brothers and sisters are sometimes tested, as a matter of routine. Some of them are found to have the disease also, even though they do not appear to be severely affected. CF mainly affects the way in which the lungs and digestive system work, but some other organs may also be affected. Although it is known that only one pair of genes causes CF, its effects are felt in many parts of the body which at first seem to be unrelated. What links them is the presence of secretory glands. Most of the effects of CF seem to result from the production of abnormally thick or dry secretions by many of the body's secretory organs and glands.

In the lungs this means that the mucus or sputum is very thick, difficult to remove, and easily infected. Sometimes the mucus blocks the tiny tubules through which air has to pass during breathing. This can lead to lung damage when air passes the mucus on breathing in, but cannot pass on breathing out. Lung damage is also caused through the invasion of the mucus by various bacteria. People with CF usually have regular antibiotic therapy to prevent this. It is generally felt that it is better to prevent infections occurring than to wait until they are established and then try to treat them.

The digestive system is also affected. In many children it is the digestive problems which alert their parents and doctors to the presence of CF long before any respiratory problems arise. A small number of babies are born with an obstruction caused by CF called *Meconium Ileus*. This means that the meconium, a substance which is contained in the gut of all newborn babies, is unusually thick and dry. Instead of being passed by the baby as its first "dirty" nappy, it forms an obstruction which often has to be removed surgically. This is an indication that the CF digestive problems begin before birth.

The organ which is most affected is the pancreas. This produces a digestive juice which helps digest all three major components of a diet – carbohydrate, protein and fat. Because of CF, the ducts through which the digestive juice should emerge become blocked, and the pancreas itself is progressively destroyed.

This inability to digest food properly, as well as other changes in the gut, mean that people with CF are unable to absorb those nutrients which have been digested. Two things become obvious in children who have CF: they produce unpleasant, smelly and bulky faeces, and they do not grow at the expected rate for their age and family in spite of being continually hungry.

Other glands are changed, but their effects do not usually cause any problems. The secretions from the salivary glands are often thicker, and the sweat glands produce a much saltier secretion than in other people. Children who have CF are more likely to suffer in hot countries or during heatwaves from "heat-exhaustion" due to loss of salt. It is this salty sweat which forms the basis of the most common test for CF. Many mothers of CF babies have said that they noticed how salty their babies tasted when kissed! Most CF males are sterile, because of damage caused by the disease to the sperm-carrying tubules in their reproductive organs. Fertility in females is not affected in this way, although pregnancy could have a serious effect on the health of many CF women.

There is no cure for CF at present. Recently there has been a great deal of research in many countries into the way in which the recessive gene causes the changes which are characteristic of CF. At the same time there have been many advances in the treatment of people who have CF.

During the early years after the recognition of CF as a particular disease in the late 1930s, life expectancy was very short. Before that time we have no idea how many children were born with CF, since most of them died very young from "lung infections" or "digestive problems". At the present time, treatment is aimed at minimising long-term damage to the parts of the body affected by CF, while ensuring the patient keeps as healthy as possible and leads as full and normal a life as he or she can. Most people who have CF are under the care of a specialist. A few people are under the care of a special CF centre at a hospital. Most patients have regular check-ups at which their growth and development are monitored, their lung function is checked, and they get advice from a specialist physiotherapist and dietitian. Their doctor monitors their general health and well-being and may make recommendations for changes in treatment. The day-to-day routine for CF patients usually includes physio, exercise, drugs such as bronchodilators, which help to keep the lung passages open, antibiotics, vitamin supplements, and enzyme supplements to help digest food. This may seem like a very heavy regime, especially for a young child, but for those children who have CF it is literally their way of life. Doctors usually advise immunisation against the common childhood diseases, but when a child with CF does get ill it usually means stepping up the existing regime, and sometimes admission to hospital is necessary. There is a great variation in the severity of such infections from child to child.

Thanks to the many advances in treatment over the last twenty or so years, and the development of enzyme preparations which enable children to be much better nourished and fit, a much greater proportion of the babies born with CF are now surviving to adulthood. There is now a CF Adults Association in the UK whose members are increasing in number all the time. Research continues in the hope of identifying the abnormal or missing biochemical substance which is the underlying cause of the disease. At the same time, tests are being developed to identify carriers of the gene, and to detect it in unborn babies.

The Cystic Fibrosis Research Trust

Since its foundation in 1964 the Trust's aims and objectives have been, and still are:
1. To finance research to find a complete cure – and in the meantime, to improve upon current methods of treatment.
2. To establish Branches and Groups throughout the UK for the purpose of helping and advising parents with the everyday problems of caring for those affected with Cystic Fibrosis.
3. To educate the public about Cystic Fibrosis and through wider knowledge help to promote earlier diagnosis in young children.

Over 100 Councils, Regions and Branches, and 250 Groups, are now active throughout the UK.

The Trust's Research & Medical Advisory Committee has allocated over 300 Grants to medical and scientific projects based in hospitals and universities in all parts of Great Britain and Northern Ireland.

The Trust's magazine, CFNEWS, reaches over 20,000 homes, together with the newspaper CFNOW.

A Welfare Office gives expert advice to all those involved in the care of those with Cystic Fibrosis. The Trust also supports and sponsors the Association of CF Adults.

Contact this address for details:
Cystic Fibrosis Research Trust
Alexandra House
5 Blyth Road
Bromley
Kent BR1 3RS
Tel: 01-464 7211

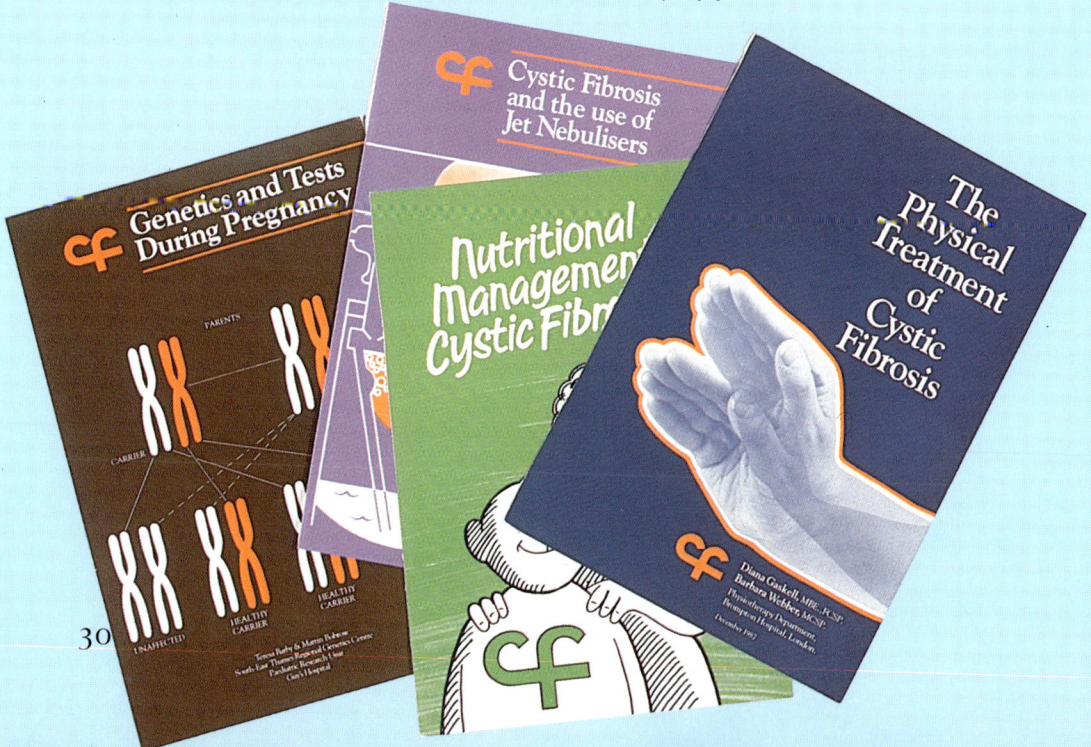

Glossary

Antibiotic A substance which is used to kill bacteria in the body. Most antibiotics are either taken by mouth, as tablets, capsules or liquids, or they are injected.

Bronchodilator A substance which causes the "bronchi" (the tubes which carry air into the lungs) to dilate, or grow wider. This makes breathing easier, especially if the tubes have become clogged with mucus.

Dietitian A person who has been trained to advise on all matters concerned with diet and nutrition.

Digestion The process by which complex food substances are broken down in the digestive tract into simple chemicals such as glucose, amino acids, fatty acids and glycerol. These simple substances are then able to travel in the bloodstream to those parts of the body where they are needed.

Enzymes Chemicals produced by living organisms whose function is to enable chemical reactions to take place. In the digestive system, enzymes enable the complex food substances which are eaten to be broken down into simpler ones.

Gene The "instruction" found in the nucleus of each living cell, for a single inherited characteristic. Most characteristics are controlled by pairs of genes. For a recessive characteristic to manifest itself, both genes must carry that characteristic. The opposite of "recessive" is "dominant". A dominant gene will affect the person carrying it even if only one of a pair of genes has it.

Mucus The secretion of glands in mucous membranes. This occurs on most of the internal surfaces of the body. Normally, mucus is colourless and slightly thicker than saliva.

Nebuliser A device which makes a mist out of a liquid by blowing air or oxygen through it. It can be used to deliver various medicines directly to the lungs.

Pancreas A gland which is found under the stomach in humans. It produces a digestive juice which is secreted into the gut, and insulin which is passed directly into the bloodstream.

Physiotherapy This is the use of massage, exercises and sometimes heat treatment to treat people who are suffering from disease, injury or deformity. A person who is specially trained to do this is called a "physiotherapist".

Index

Antibiotics 12, 27, 29, 31

"Banging" 8
Bronchodilator 29, 31

CF Adults Association 29, 30
Capsules 15, 16, 31
"Carriers" 27, 31
Cystic Fibrosis Research Trust 21, 22, 30

Diet 14, 17, 23, 28, 31
Digestion 14, 31
Digestive system 18, 27, 28, 31
Doctor 6, 7, 25, 29, 31

Exercise 9, 19, 20, 23, 29, 31

Fat 14, 15, 16, 28
Food 7, 14, 15, 28, 29, 31
Fund-raising 21, 22

Gene 6, 27, 29, 31
Glands 27, 28, 31

Hospital 7, 8, 13, 29, 30, 31
"Huffing" 10

Infection 8, 11, 27, 29

Lungs 8, 9, 10, 11, 12, 20, 27, 28, 29, 31

Mucus 8, 9, 10, 11, 27, 31

Nebuliser 12, 13, 24, 31

Pancreas 28, 31
Parents 6, 7, 8, 22, 26, 27, 30
Physiotherapy 8, 9, 23, 29, 31

"Sputum" 11, 27
"Sweat test" 7

The Handi-Read logo appears only on those books and audio-visual items approved by the national Library for the Handicapped Child, sponsored by The Enid Blyton Trust for Children.

The Handi-Read logo may not be reproduced, stored in a retrieval system or transmitted by any means, electronic, mechanical, photocopying, recording or otherwise, without the prior permission of The Enid Blyton Trust For Children.